IF YOU TEND TO GHOST PEOPLE, THINK AGAIN:
11 Things Ghosting Says About You

Amber S. McKim

Table Of Contents

What Type of Person is a Ghoster?

Those who ghost more frequently have avoidant, manipulative, and self-centered personality and behavioral qualities.

"You might want to ask yourself if this is likely to happen with you too," she advises. "If you find trends of regularly ending relationships without resolution and/or quitting jobs without first providing feedback to remedy concerns, then you might want to ask yourself." "I would also be wary of anyone who seems to have hidden intentions for becoming too close, too quickly, and/or if they tend to want to know much more about you personally than you know about them,"

The first thing that has to be addressed is that although ghosting is cruel, it doesn't make you a bad person and isn't the ideal method to end a relationship. Nothing prevents you from making better decisions going forward by using the lessons you've learned from past errors.

There is no one particular type of person who ghosts. One gender is not more affected by it than the other.

Anybody can ghost someone. However, it is associated with several general personality features. Although not all of these may apply to you explicitly, one or a few probably may.
Ghosters are not always simple to identify. So here are some unusual personality qualities that, according to experts, can indicate if someone will ghost their way out of a relationship.

- **Commitment issues.** For whatever reason,You just don't feel comfortable committing to one person, for whatever reason. You prefer to maintain a range of alternatives while excluding others. You favor casual, low-commitment partnerships.

- **Self-centered.** Relationships are reciprocal. It's acceptable to express your requirements and goals clearly. However, being overly preoccupied with oneself and failing to recognize how you affect others raises a warning signal.

- **Secretive.** It's okay to have some mystery in a relationship. It may even be seductive. Even though the other person gives a lot of information about themselves, you conceal yourself and share very little about yourself.

- **Passive.** While it's normal to want to avoid awkward circumstances or harming other people, doing so increases your likelihood of ghosting. It is practical and uses less time and effort.

- **Fickle.** People frequently change their opinions. It is in our nature. But it takes work to let someone know you're no longer interested in them. If you unexpectedly change your mind or emotions, you are more likely to ghost someone.

- **They Lack Awareness.**

Ghosting doesn't just happen to those in more recent relationships. After being in a relationship for a while, some people do leave. People who are likely to ghost their long-term spouses may lack empathy or awareness, according to Josephson. She writes, "I try to avoid pathologizing, but I can't help but feel that this person's decision to ghost after a substantial engagement is a massive red flag and warning that this person is not capable of seeing any relationship through or being a good partner." They could also generally be "very deficient" in empathy and social skills.

Is Ghosting Abusive?

Ghosting has been characterized by some mental health specialists as a passive-aggressive form of emotional abuse or cruelty since it has been linked to detrimental mental health impacts on the person receiving it.

Preventing emotional distress in a relationship is the most frequent reason for ghosting in intimate relationships. Ghosters frequently give little thought to how their actions will affect the other person.

The existence of toxic or violent relationships may be the lone factor increasing the acceptability of ghosting.

Any form of disrespect is unpleasant. It's better to address the concerns and make it clear to the other person that you don't want to have any more contact with them unless you are concerned for your safety.

In other words, ghosting is harmful unless you're doing it to get away from an abusive partner.

Ghosting a person you care about is:

- **Painful.** When you disappear without a trace, the person you ghost feels degraded, disposable, and irrelevant. Since the same brain regions are engaged, the resulting pain can be just as acute as physical pain. It hurts worse than breaking up face to face certainly.

- Many ghostees are unsure of how to handle being abandoned without warning. They experience insecurity and a sense of unworthiness. It may affect one's self-worth, self-esteem, and confidence.

- **lacking completion.** It's confusing if you don't explain why you're ending the relationship. They start to question what went wrong and what is wrong with them as a result. Additionally, it hinders individuals from reflecting on their errors and figuring out how to avoid repeating them in the future.

- **Traumatic.** Being abruptly cut off without warning can stoke fresh wounds or reopen old ones. Being ghosted can make mental health problems like anxiety, sadness, and other concerns worse, especially if the person being ghosted already has attachment, abandonment, or mental health problems.

- **With malice.** Your silence kills the ghostee's desire to form new relationships, platonic or otherwise, whether you ghost them in short-term, long-term, or friendship partnerships. They become distrustful and become stuck in the past, wondering what they did to deserve such harsh treatment.

What Ghosting Says About You: 11 Not-So-Great Things

You know you ghosted someone, after all.
Ideally, you want to correct your errors and stop that pattern.

These may be difficult to hear, but realizing WHY you act a certain way can help you develop better skills for politely ending a relationship that is no longer beneficial to you.

Or perhaps you've been ghosted and are attempting to understand what happened.

Here are a few traits that ghosters frequently have.

1. You have a fear of confrontation.

Feelings can be confusing and disorganized. Instead of having a difficult talk about why you're ending it, especially one that can result in tears and wounded sentiments, it might seem easier to simply vanish.

By ghosting, you avoid having to deal with the fallout or consoling people's shattered egos.

However, you are aware that the wisest course of action is not to ignore or pretend that their injured sentiments aren't there.

2. You think it's normal.

Ghosting has become more common as online dating and social media have grown in popularity. It's well-known and well-liked.

The pool of potential partners appears to be limitless. You stop answering calls and texts and might even block them because there are many other people to select from if it doesn't work out with the first one.

It may be more widespread now, but that doesn't make it morally good.

3. You lack emotional intelligence

The capacity to understand, control, and manage your own emotions as well as those of others while positively influencing others is known as emotional intelligence.

Lack of emotional intelligence results in a lack of empathy, which makes it difficult to resolve conflicts, communicate clearly, and accept responsibility for your actions.

For yourself and the people around you, what you say and do matters. It doesn't imply it doesn't happen just because you don't see their hurt reaction..

4. Your communication skills are lacking.

Maybe you were never taught how to express your needs, wants, and desires in a conversation. Or perhaps you become so reliant on internet communication because of its rising popularity of it that you lost the ability to communicate effectively.

Forming relationships is more difficult while communicating through a screen, and you can generally say whatever you want without having to worry about their hurt feelings.

sobbing woman chatting on the phone ghosting: What it says about you

Even if you don't have a connection to the victim of your actions, doing so is still wrong.

5. You have immature relationship patterns.

Ghosting is immature, to be honest. Perhaps you unwittingly picked up the habit of ghosting people as a child, or it could be a self-defense tactic.

Whatever your motivations, it's irresponsible not to think about how your actions may affect the other person.

This unhealthy behavior harms the other person and prevents you from forging deep connections with others.

If you don't think you can handle it on your own, think about getting a professional's assistance.

6. You're trying to avoid negative feelings.

It's no secret that terminating a relationship is difficult, whether you're the one doing it or the other person is doing it to you. It frequently entails discomfort and agony.

Nobody enjoys experiencing sadness, and most people don't enjoy making others feel unhappy. However, if you believe that ghosting enables you to avoid that sort of uncomfortable emotion, think again. If you ghost once, you probably won't stop. This starts a vicious cycle that is difficult to escape.

7. You're cowardly.

You lack the guts to inform someone you are ghosting
them in person. Being unwilling to accept responsibility is
weak and reveals your vulnerabilities.

Harsh? Maybe. True? Definitely.

Instead of ghosting someone you're no longer interested in
dating, respect your relationship with them, however
fleeting it may be, and give them closure. Have the guts to
appropriately reject the other person.

8. You're disrespectful.

Ghosting someone you supposedly care about is impolite and disrespectful. You are intentionally causing another person pain.

Maybe all you wanted was to gain something from it, and when you did, you left without even saying goodbye. Consider your feelings if the circumstances were reversed. Wouldn't it be better if the other person respected you enough to explain why they no longer needed you in their life?

9. You have an avoidant attachment style.

When it comes to relationships, your attachment style is quite telling. You can be the avoidant type if you avoid being among people who are emotionally connected to you.

weeping woman after reading texts ghosting: What it says about you

Perhaps you struggle with commitment and are unwilling or unable to settle down. That is entirely OK. Ghosting is not, though.

Although intimacy can be frightening, that is not a reason to ghost someone. It's not a very good one, at least.

10. You have a fixed mindset.

Either people have a fixed attitude or a growth mindset. People who have a growth mentality think that maintaining healthy relationships requires efforts to overcome inescapable differences.

They don't hold their partner's personality responsible for issues, nor do they anticipate constant magic in the relationship.

On the other side, if you have a fixed attitude, you probably think either it's meant to be or it's not. You probably don't think that relationships require work or that you and your spouse can develop a loving connection via effort and effective communication.

You want to go rather than strive to improve it since you believe in destiny and this isn't yours.

11. It's a power play.

Ghosting someone might make you feel in control and perhaps make you feel proud of yourself. Because you are frightened of being rejected yourself, you reject others before they can reject you.

An indication of insecurity is this. Ghosting may give you a false sense of security and brief emotions of superiority, but it does not elevate you above other people. Instead, it's a vicious circle that is harmful to all parties.

The next time you think about ghosting someone, stop and imagine what it might be like for them. Take into account their feelings as well as the aftereffects of losing someone.

To understand why you want to ghost them, do some introspection. Find a more responsible method to end the relationship after that.

Do Ghosters Feel Guilty?

It stings to be ghosted. It's upsetting, disconcerting, and makes it challenging to establish trust in upcoming relationships since you constantly wonder if the next person will vanish as well.

Do ghosters ever feel bad about what they've done? We are aware that ghosting reveals much more about the ghoster than the ghostee.

Do you care?

Let's start now.

Do people who ghost others feel bad about it? Sometimes. According to a recent survey of mostly female college students, 65% of those who ghosted reported feeling some degree of anxiety and remorse about what they had done. Surprisingly, a lot of the fear was related to bumping into that person again or running into them on social media.

However, feeling guilty about ghosting doesn't always result in remorse for the action.

In their eyes, ghosting someone rather than outright rejecting them is more considerate. Anyone who has experienced ghosting, however, is aware that this is untrue.

Particularly intriguing is the way that chronic ghosters express their remorse. If you read a ghosting essay or think piece, you'll see a pattern:

Many ghosters, especially repeat offenders, believe that they did nothing wrong and that ghosting is a gentle way to end a relationship.

If they feel any guilt, they will deal with it by acting even more avoidantly, such as blocking the person they ghosted on social media.

To avoid being exposed or questioned about their ghosting activity, they will say or do anything. Their guilt is not motivated by sympathy for the victim of their wrongdoing.

Ghosting typically stems from inexperience and fear.
Usually, those who ghost do so out of a fear of conflict.
In the aforementioned study, respondents stated that they ghosted because they didn't want to offend the ghostee.
They're trying to express that they don't want to see someone else harm their feelings.

The ghostee will suffer harm and be left with unanswered questions; this is especially harmful to young individuals who are still learning how to build healthy relationships.

That conduct demonstrates a lack of maturity and utter disregard for the other person.

A ghoster's life will gradually incorporate into other areas.

By avoiding opportunities to establish emotional closeness and trust via constructive disagreement, the ghoster misses out on developing important life skills that will aid them in their personal and professional goals.

It entails being unable to handle disagreements or having unpleasant conversations, both of which are inevitable as an adult.

Why Ghosting Hurts Both the Ghoster and the Ghostee

Many people mistakenly think that the harm is a one-way street.
It's gotten exceedingly simple for someone to leave another person hanging in relationships in the current era—and yeah, not just romantic ones. Simply stop responding to them, unfollow them on all relevant social media platforms, and ban them.

Ghosting has increased in popularity as a result of this. Most of us either know someone who has ghosted someone or have ghosted someone ourselves.

When I mentioned that ghosting also had a negative impact on the ghoster's mental health in a conversation with a friend, he appeared perplexed. Then I realized that many people agree with him.

Contrary to popular belief, ghosting may be just as hurtful to the person who "ghosts" as it is to the person who is left behind. As the proverb goes, for every finger you point at someone else, three are pointing back at you.

A quick disclaimer: I am not referring to cases in which someone ghosts someone else because they are being stalked, persistently pursued after receiving a clear rejection, or put in a risky or uncomfortable scenario. Ghosting is entirely appropriate in these situations. I'm referring to instances where someone abruptly and without warning ends a conversation with another person in order to avoid having a difficult (but essential) topic.

So let's discuss what goes wrong in both directions.

The Ghostee

The harm done to the recipient—hereafter referred to as the ghostee—is quite obvious. Most often, people are utterly taken by surprise by the lack of communication since they believe their relationship is going well. They don't get any answers, leaving them to ponder what they did wrong. It could be a trying emotional experience that makes it harder for them to trust people in the future.

This happened to one of my close friends while she was a freshman. His girlfriend of a few months abruptly stopped reacting to him when summer arrived. Since everything appeared to be going well for them, I was astounded. He ultimately got over it, but when he talked to me about it afterwards, his perplexity was clear:

Yes, I tried phoning and texting her, but she simply stopped answering. I'm not sure what happened because everything seemed to be okay to me.

Although you can't hear his voice, you would be certain of how much it wounded him if you could.

The Ghoster

Let's now focus on the ghoster, who many people tend to ignore. What harm does the person who ghosts suffer? Although it may appear that they have protected their feelings by avoiding a difficult topic, this might also injure them in the long run.

The ghoster continues a pattern of handling their emotions in an unhealthy way by failing to express their emotions clearly. Guilt and humiliation may be the result of this. I still experience periodic regret for ghosting a friend five years ago when I might have simply had an open discussion with them.

Additionally, the more often they do this, the more probable it is that they will persuade themselves that this is a workable answer. Recall my friend from up there? I heard the female he was dating's side of the story in great detail because she is also a good friend of mine.

She described how she was able to detect that the two of them weren't compatible. She could have just told him the truth, but since they would be apart for the summer anyhow, she thought that this was the best course of action. It would have been healthier emotionally for them both.

She has ghosted other people besides just him. Although I consider her to be a fantastic friend, I'd be lying if I said it didn't irritate me to see her repeat this behavior. It is never successful. Everyone, including her, is dealing with unresolved emotions and damaged feelings.

What You Can Do Instead

Ghosting can sometimes be harmful behavior. However, ghosting is rarely a good idea beyond that. The other person suffers, becoming lost and perplexed as a result. If you are a nice person, it burdens your conscience and feeds a destructive cycle of denying your feelings.

What then should you do in its place? Well, being honest is the best course of action. Be compassionate but tough. In case you need some inspiration, consider these two real-world examples:

1. For a few weeks, my cousin had been speaking with a man, but it didn't seem like a good fit. You're a gem of a person, but we desire different things in life, he finally said to her. brief and sweet In fact, she had been experiencing the same things.

2. If being that direct is difficult for you, you can go about it a little differently. For example, one of my friends didn't know how to tell a girl he was no longer

interested after one date, so he still responded politely
and respectfully, but without any signs of romance or
a desire to meet up again. As she is obviously the more
emotionally mature of the two, she ultimately caught
the signal and questioned him directly if he was
interested or not. He then acknowledged that he
wasn't.
Although Option 1 is superior than Option 2, both are
preferable to ghosting.

In conclusion, avoid ghosting. It may eventually cause
harm to you as well.

www.ingramcontent.com/pod-product-compliance
Lightning Source LLC
Chambersburg PA
CBHW060928130726
48001CB00006B/2474